自由学園明日館

フランク・ロイド・ライト

重要文化財
東京 1921

解説│谷川正己　撮影│宮本和義

Frank Lloyd Wright
Jiyu Gakuen, School of The Free Sprit
Myonichikan
Tokyo 1921

Text: Masami Tanigawa　Photos: Kazuyoshi Miyamoto

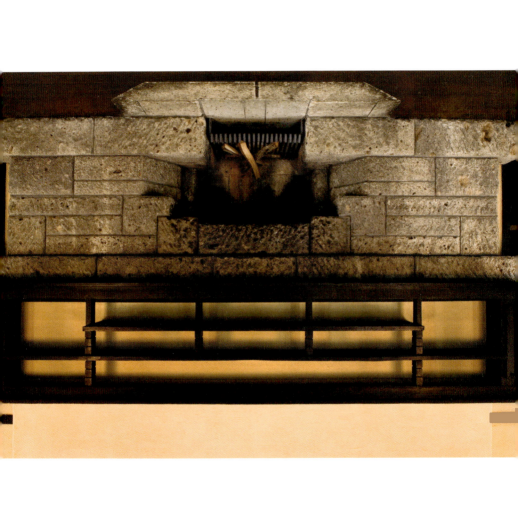

目次

明日館写真	4-27
図面	28-31
ディティール	32-37
守り継ぐライトの遺産	
住宅街に潜む	40
軽快な空間構成	42
伝統工法とライト	46
大地と繋がる床	48
意志を継ぐ弟子	50
巨匠への依頼	52
完成前に行われた落成式	54
残された図面と未完の校舎	56
昭和の文化財指定第一号	58
動態保存への試み	60
蘇る美しい姿	62

フランク・ロイド・ライト

自由学園明日館
東京 1921

Frank Lloyd Wright
Jiyu Gakuen, School of The Free Sprit
Myonichikan
Tokyo 1921

Text: Masami Tanigawa　　Photos: Kazuyoshi Miyamoto

Photos of the Jiyu Gakuen	4-27
Drawings	28-31
Details	32-37
Inheriting Wright's Heritage	
Hiding in Residential Ares	41
Swinging Spatial Composition	43
Traditional Construction Methods and Wright	47
Floors Connected to the Ground	49
Apprentice Inheriting Wright,s heritage	51
Request for a Maestro of Architecture	53
Completion Ceremony before the Completion	55
Left Drawings and Unfinished School Buildings	57
First Registration as a Cultual Property in the showa Priod	59
Trial for Dynamic Conservation	61
Revitalized Beauty	63

70

アトリエ-2の外観。東、西教室棟の両端の建屋は芝生の庭に張り出している。全体の半俯瞰を引き当てている。左隅にゲートが半分見えている。

Appearance of the Atelier 2. The south ends of both the east and west classroom buildings stick out onto the grassy lawn, as well as tone up the total plan. A part of the gate is seen on the left.

キャンパスの建築群の顔。2階部分を張り出すホールの外観。ライト氏、母校ラスキン高等学校のファサードを、ガラス、鉛の棒、色付けしたベニヤ板を取り付けるという、曲面でもあまり高くない手法で飾った。彼は修復工事で、ライトのオリジナルデザインに忠実に修復され、彼の非凡なデザインが実感できることとなった。

The face of the buildings of the campus. Appearance of the 2-story hall. Wright decorated the facade at a low cost, high quality method; colored glass fixed by lead bars similar to stained glass and the occasional use of plywood. The restoration work of the building to the original design of Wright makes us realize his marvelous design skills.

中央棟中央部は地面よりも少し高い。階段の踏面は3枚、最初の蹴上げは極端に低い。そもそも敷石舗装の原石の表石は、床面より少々嵩上げされたらしい。

The central part of the building is a little higher than ground level. There are 3 treads and the first riser is extremely low. The paving stones on the lawn were said to be slightly raised after construction.

西校舎の外観。教室棟の廊下には列柱様式が並ぶ。列柱は柱ではなく、張り詰められた桂壁なのだが、その大きな陰影を取り囲む庭を一層引き立てている。

Appearance of the west classroom building. There is a row of columns. These columns are not structural columns but formed patterns. The width of these columns makes the scenery surrounding the garden more attractive.

西校舎の外廊下。列柱の織りなす陰影が美しい。教室の床、廊下の敷石、そして芝生の庭が同一のレベルにある。やはり国で建造に行かれる履物の着脱が必ずしも必要国ではなく、こちらが内外とも一体になっているのであろう。

Hallway of the west classroom building. Even the shadows of the columns are beautiful. The floors of the classrooms, the stone pavement of the hallway and the lawn, are all on the same level. This would be more attuned with the integration of the inside and the outside as in the USA, where it is unnecessary to put on and take off footwear.

中央校舎棟への玄関。ガラス張りの扉にも、その上部、
欄間のサッシ割にも、枠に共通のデザインで、細部にも気
遣いを凝らしている。

Entrance to the classrooms of the main building. The same design of sash bars is adopted for the glazed door and the upper side of the door. All the details are filled with care.

階下からの中央校舎棟への玄関を望む。芝生の庭と玄関、廊下
に段差はない。目線、大地との一体感がある。雨天の日には
木種や靴の水滴が持ち込まれてしまうことになる。

Looking at the entrance from the hallway to the classrooms of the main building. The lawn, the entrance and the hallway are at the same level. There is a sense of unity with nature and earth, though, water droplets on clothes and footwear would be brought inside on a rainy day.

西校舎棟の廊下の天窓。正方形の枠を45度傾け、
桟割も幾何学的な割り付けがされている。対応するはずある
の東校舎棟廊下の天窓は、これとはまったく異なる
デザインのものとなっている。

Top light of the hallway of the west classroom building. The frame of a square shape is angled at 45 degrees and the sash bars are geometrically designed. The possible counterpart, the top light on the hallway of the east classroom building has a totally different design.

中央棟校舎第 1 教室内。開校式に間に合わせるために建設された最初の教室。式当日の写真には、壁は漆喰の状態であり、モルタル仕上げは、天井とともに漆喰塗り。廊下を挟んだ反対側の教室は、船底天井のために天井が高く広い、実際は軽く感じられるのだ。電灯は、当初的に教室には電気配線は無かった。後ほど取り付けられ、日没前には生徒たちをホームに帰らせていたようだ。

The west side classroom-1 of the main building, inside. The first classroom constructed in order to be in time for the opening ceremony of the school. The walls were scratch coat, which we can see in the photographs of the ceremony. Both the walls and the ceiling are finished with stucco.
The classrooms after the hallway with a low ceiling, seem larger, lighter and higher than the actual measurements, because the rooms have ceilings shaped like the hull of a ship... The lighting equipment was installed later on. Basically, there was no electric wiring. They say students, after school, were to go home before dark.

中央南東端-3年内。それぞれの教室の室内外周には柱はない。建物の天井と違って教室の天井は、天井の形によって異なる異型各教室は、棟、天井による連続感より仕上げが重要、これは室内が東側になるために、目刷り様が多用されている。

The east side classroom-3 of the main building. The classrooms do not necessarily have the same interior. The inside space vary according to the scale or the shape of the ceiling. The walls and the ceiling of each classroom are basically finished with stucco. This monotonizes the interior space, therefore, lining sash bars are often used.

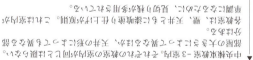

中央講堂ホール、真奥への玄関内廊下。廊下の両側には下駄箱、傘立てが造り付けになっている。

Entrance hallway to the dining room and the lounge hall of the main building. The footwear cupboard and the umbrella stands are built-in on the both sides.

中央講堂ホール。キャンパスの中で最も広い、2階吹き抜けの空間はドラマチックな雰囲気にまとめられている。暖炉を中心に和洋折衷の暖かみのある意匠。

一階2階のギャラリーはほど広くはないが、見下ろす視点の使用には甚だ楽な空間である。前川創生はそれに適した幾何学モチーフの下での使用が目的的のものであり、一階階段下での家具調度の種々の状況を観察する為に点。講堂が落成工事までの開は、もちろん礼儀作法を学ぶなど情操教育の場としても使われた。

中央講堂ホールの階下から続きの階下を含む位置に設置されたれた天窓と電灯を併用、幾何学的な棒が用意されている。

Lounge hall of the main building. This is the largest room in the campus. The space with a 2-story height has a dramatic design. There is a cozy atmosphere with the fireplace in the center. Although the gallery on the 2nd floor is not large, it would be valuable for viewing the downstairs hall. All lighting equipment has a geometric design. The hall is for meetings as well as for educating homey manners. This hall was used for ritual functions until the auditorium was completed.

Top lighting is set where we can see the classroom's hallway from the main building's hallway. Both the natural light and the electric lights are used in combination. Geometric sash bars are used.

015

中央棟ホール。西側壁面のフレスコ画。戦災復旧工事で壁体中、上塗りの下から この壁画が現れた。縦2.5m、横5.0mの壁画で、旧約聖書「出エジプト記第十三章」を題材としたものという。太平洋戦争中に不穏当な画題という事で壁面が塗りつぶされていたらしい。学園創立10周年記念には生徒たちによって描かれた フレスコ画は修復工事中に撤去した。壁画の左手奥には塗られている肖像も創立 創生記念に生徒たちが描いた。

中央棟ホールから庭を望む。特有の美しい開口がホールと庭の調和に寄 与する。ここは内と外とが一体感を味わえる 贅沢な空間ということになろうか。

The mural on the west wall of the hall. This was discovered beneath the face coating during the restoration. At a size of 5.0m (width) × 2.5m (height). Its theme comes from "Exodus:13" of the Old Testament. They say it was concealed beneath thick mortar because the theme of this mural was ill advised during World War II. This mural, painted by students, commemorates the 10th anniversary of the founding of the Jiyu Gakuen School. The statue in the left before the mural was also by students from the 10th anniversary.

Looking at the garden from the main building. The enormous, beautiful, opening contributes to the integration of the hall and the garden. This might be a place where we can feel a sense of the unity of inside and outside.

遠藤設計の小食堂附属部分の詳細。窓の桟の太さが他の部分と異なる。東、西、北の3方にも食堂がある。

Details of the small dining annex designed by Arata Endo. The width of the window sash bars is different from that of other parts. These small dining rooms are on the north, east and west.

中央食堂へは、内廊下から階段を上り、まずギャラリーへと客を寄せる階段を上らなければならない。それぞれに特徴的な眺望が得られる。特に食堂上の世界を体験することになる。到着した瞬間から、装飾的な視線は、食堂へのアプローチで頭を押え、パッと広がる客席の装飾的に誇張されるだろうというライトの演出。

We have to walk up the stairs from the inside hallway to the dining room as well as from the dining room to the gallery. Each has only a half story, but we can experience distinctive views with the difference in levels. The box at the corner of the room is a gimmick by Wright so that the dining space would dramatically expand after the low ceiling at the approach to the room.

中央食堂は、いわば本校舎たちが家で作った様々な学芸、生産の品々を食する空間。食事の空間は華やかというより、むしろ厳粛で端正な場であろう。生徒たちは食事の作法を実践的に習得している。暖炉、飾りの付いた窓、調度品、卓、椅子などがそれぞれ模園良い雰囲気を醸し出している。

The dining hall of the main building. In this space, all the teachers and the students had meals prepared by the students, in turn. The dining space would be a dignified ceremonial place, rather than an aesthetic one. Students learned practical dining manners. A magnificent atmosphere is created with the fireplace, the decorated windows, the lighting, the tables and the chairs.

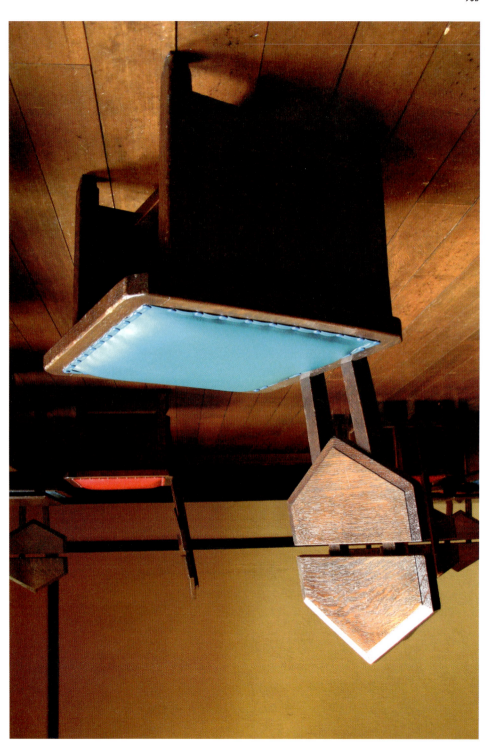

▼ ライト設計の帝国ホテルの椅子を取って、六角形を踏襲とした椅子。しかし、制作時期や設計者は未詳。ラワン材使用。背もたれは六角形、座面はレザート。

Chairs with a hexagonal back, similar to the ones of the Imperial Hotel designed by Wright. However, it is unknown when or by whom these chairs were made. Made of lauan. The backs have a shape of hexagons and the seats are of leather.

▼ 1922年7月、帝国ホテルでは「ライト送別会」が催された。帝国ホテルも自由学園も工事途中の組を決断したライトの心境はいろいろ複雑なものであったろう。ライトの右側に遠藤新夫子、右手に涼籐を持つ遠藤も見える。

In July 1922, they held a farewell party for Wright. He might have had mixed feelings because he had decided to leave Japan in the midst of the construction of both the Imperial Hotel and the Jiyu Gakuen School. Motoko Hani is seen at the right in front of Wright and Arata Endo also on the right in the photograph.

025

上：講堂北東側外観
下：講堂東側外観

Above: Northeast appearance of the auditorium entrance
Below: East facade of the auditorium

講堂は遠藤新建築設計。竣工は1927年6月のこと。昭和時代に入って、すべての建築が竣工も時ったことになる。講堂はこのキャンパスの中でもっとも新しい建築だが、それでも築170年以上経過している。しかし、継続的な維持があるからこそ、現状を変更せず、建ち続けている。文化財指定後の保存修理工事でも、講堂は届出外として、修理されることはなかった。

The auditorium was designed by Arata Endo and completed in June 1927. This was the last of all the planned buildings of the school. The completion year was the 2nd year of the Showa period. Although the auditorium was the most recently constructed, more than 70 years have passed since it was built. Regardless of the length of time, a careful maintenance has kept the building in good condition, without change. Even during restoring construction after the registration as an important Cultural Property, the auditorium was exempted from the registration and not repaired.

上：舞台から舞台を望む。
下：舞台からギャラリーと2階客席を望む。

Above: Looking at the stage from the audience seats
Below: Looking at the gallery and the audience seats on the 2nd floor from the audience seats on the 1st floor

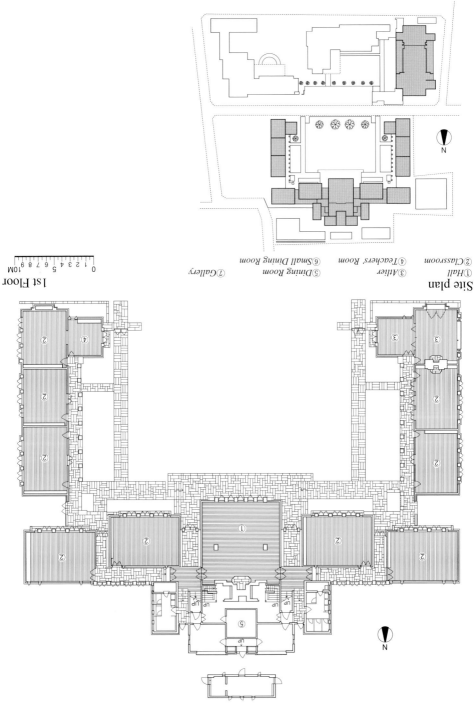

Site plan
① Hall
② Classroom
③ Atelier
④ Teacher's Room
⑤ Dining Room
⑥ Small Dining Room
⑦ Gallery

1st Floor

Floor plans

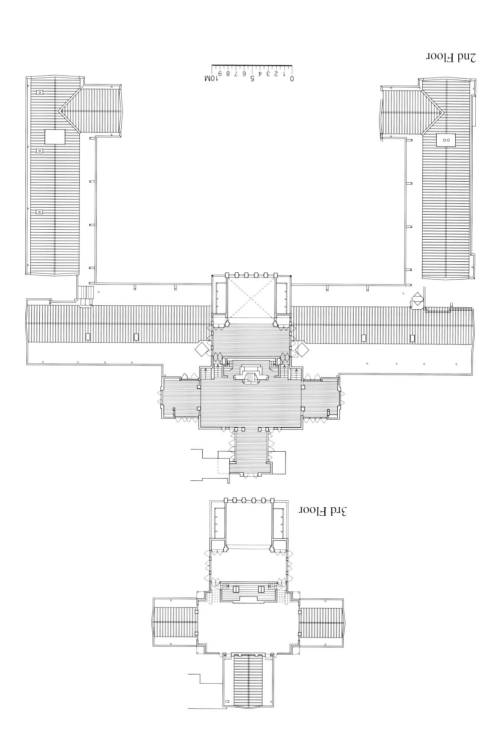

Detaild Plan of the Hall after the Re vision

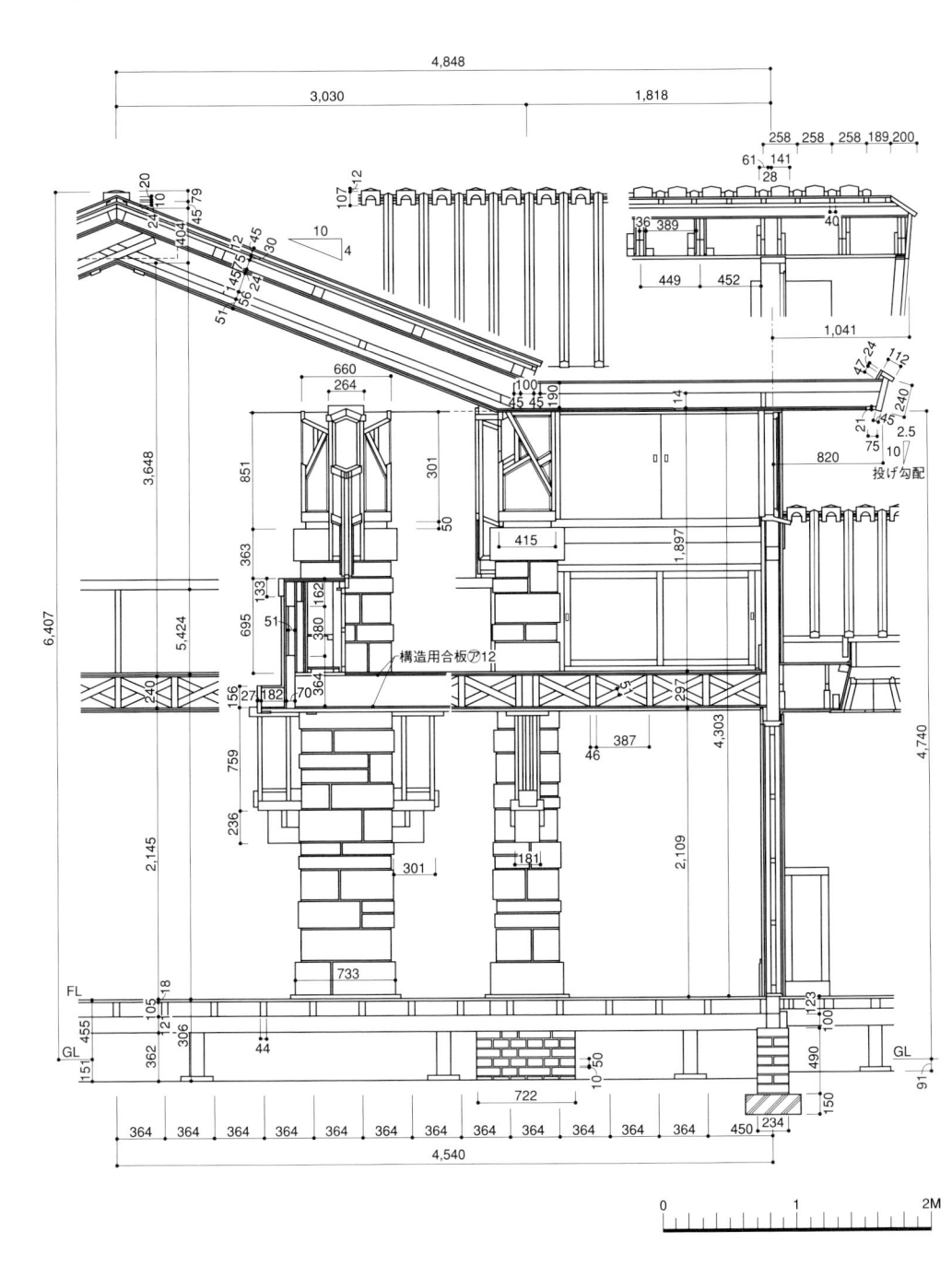

構造用合板⑦12

投げ勾配

Elevation

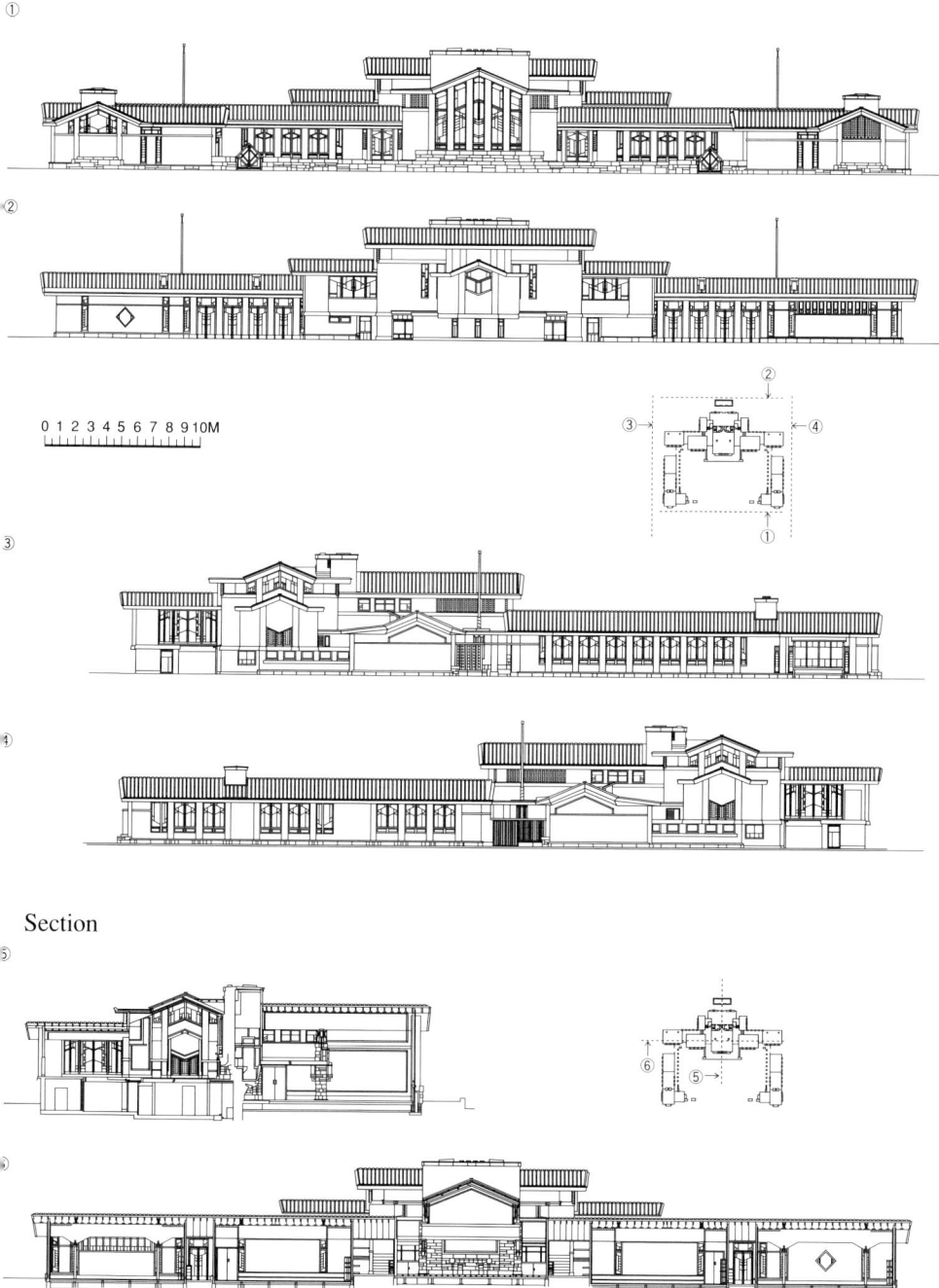

0 1 2 3 4 5 6 7 8 9 10M

Section

0 1 2 3 4 5 6 7 8 9 10M

031

Detail - 1　窓枠／Window frame

左頁上：中央棟ホールの大きい開口。木製の窓のシルエットが美しい。特に室内からの景観は四季の変化を存分に味わせてくれる。
左頁下：西教室棟アトリエ–1の南面の窓。嵌殺し故に窓のデザインの美しさを堪能できる。

右頁左上：中央棟北小食堂北面の開口。嵌殺し。遠藤設計。

右頁右上：西教室棟廊下の天窓。正方形のものだが、左右が板貼りで光を透さない。
右頁下：中央棟北食堂西面の開口。食堂からの転用。

Left page, above: large window of the hall of the main building. The silhouette of the wooden window is attractive. The view from the window brings seasonal changes into the room.
Left page, bottom: south window of the atelier-1 of the west classroom building. We can see the aesthetics of window designs particularly in these fixed windows.

Right page, above left: North window of the north dining room of the main building. Fixed. Designed by Arata Endo.

Right page, above right: Top light of the hallway of the west classroom building. It has a square shape, but both sides are boarded and do not penetrate light.
Right page, bottom: West window of the small north dining room of the main building designed by Arata Endo.

033

Detail -2　照明／Lighting Equipment

左頁左上：中央棟ホールのギャラリーを支える大谷石積みの柱上部のランタンボックス。
左頁右上：中央棟ホールのギャラリーに建つ大谷石積みの柱上部のランタンボックス。
左頁左下：中央棟食堂のペンダント。
左頁右下：中央棟東玄関前のランタンボックス。
右頁上：中央棟ホールへの玄関内廊下の天窓。

Left page, above left: Lantern box on the top of the Oya stone column supporting the gallery of the hall of the main building.
Left page, above right: Lantern box on the top of the Oya stone column standing in the gallery of the hall of the main building.
Left page, bottom left: Pendant lighting in the dining room of the main building.
Left page, bottom right: Lantern box before the east entrance of the main building.
Right page: Top light of the hallway in the entrance to the hall of the main building.

Detail - 3　木製装飾／Wood Carving

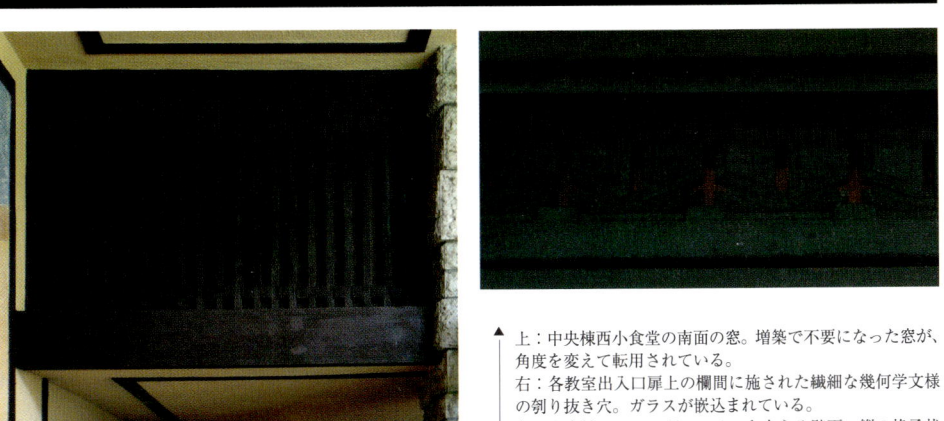

▲ 上：中央棟西小食堂の南面の窓。増築で不要になった窓が、
角度を変えて転用されている。
右：各教室出入口扉上の欄間に施された繊細な幾何学文様
の刳り抜き穴。ガラスが嵌込まれている。
左：中央棟ホールのギャラリーを支える壁面。縦の格子状
デザイン

Above: South window of the small west dining room of
the main building. The window, which became
unnecessary due to the annex, is converted here by
changing the angle.
Right: Scraped slits with detailed geometric patterns at
the fanlight on the top of the entrance door of each
classroom. The slits are glazed.
Left: Wall supporting the gallery of the hall of the main
building. Vertical grid design.

036

左：中央棟ホール外観の隅角部。柱で陸屋根を支えられているが後補のもの。竣工時に柱はなかった。

右：中央棟西教室−1の窓と軒裏換気口は、一線上に揃っている。

Left: Outside corner of the hall of the main building. The column supporting the flat roof was attached later on; there was no column at the time of completion.

Right: On the same line are the window of the west classroom1 and the ventilating hole under the eaves.

037

守り継ぐライトの遺産　　谷川正己

住宅街に潜む

　「自由学園明日館」は東京の副都心の一つ、池袋駅から500m、徒歩10分のところにある。駅周辺は高層ビルが林立し、喧噪を極めているが、わずか500m離れたここは住宅地、かつては西武電車の一つ目の「上り屋敷」（今はない）駅から武蔵野の雑木林の彼方に明日館を望見できたという。そんな情緒はもう望むべくもない。街区一杯に住宅で覆い尽され、道路は曲折していて、車は一方通行。アメリカから訪れたライト研究家を案内すると、彼らは一様に「おいおい、どこへ行こうというの？」と訝（いぶか）りながら付いてくる。重要文化財の建物に会いに行こうというのに、駅からのアプローチは余り褒められない。だが、遠藤新の次男、遠藤楽設計の婦人之友社前の三叉路を右折して、明日館の全景に接すると、これを見学に来たのだと皆納得して感動。しばらくは無言で佇むことになる。

　羽仁夫妻が低価格で造って欲しいと希求して建設されたこの建物は、質素だが清楚な子女教育の学園、格調高い雰囲気を醸し出しているのは何故か。広い芝生の庭をコの字型に囲み込んだ左右対称形の建築群。美の規範としての左右対称というのは、万人を納得させる手易くて効果のある手法。多くの権威を誇示する建物に用いられてきたが、明日館はそうした威圧感がない。それは、中心性を強調しない左右対称の造形にまとめたことにある。明日館ではゲートが2つ、中央棟の玄関は左右に2つづつ、計4カ所ある。公平性、民主的にという原則に従って造られている故に、親近感さえ味わえるということなのだろう。

ライトの日本での設計業績

1　帝国ホテル、東京、1912年
2　アメリカ大使館、東京、1914年
3　林愛作邸、東京、1917年
4　小田原ホテル、小田原、1917年
5　福原有信邸、箱根、1918年
6　井上匡四郎子爵邸、東京、1918年
7　三原邸、東京、1918年
8　映画劇場、東京、1918年
9　山邑太左衛門邸、芦屋、1918年
10　帝国ホテル別館、東京、1920年
11　後藤新平男爵邸、東京、1921年
12　自由学園、東京、1921年

他に、執行弘道邸、日比谷三角ビルディング、総理官邸など数が増える可能性がある。
ライトの国外での業績は、計画案を含めてわずか32件以上、うち日本での業績は12件以上。実現した作品数となると、日本で6、カナダで3、計9件しかない。
現存するライトの国外の作品は、日本に4件（帝国ホテル、林愛作邸、旧山邑邸、自由学園明日館）しかなく旧山邑邸とともに自由学園明日館がいかに貴重であるかがわかる。
（数値は設計年または設計開始年）

◀ ゲートは左右対称の位置に2ヶ所ある。正方形を45°傾斜させたユニークなデザイン。

There are symmetrically two gates. They have a unique design of a square angled at 45 degrees.

Wright's Architectural Achievements in Japan

1. Imperial Hotel, Tokyo, 1912
2. United States Embassy, Tokyo, 1914
3. Aisaku Hayashi House, Tokyo, 1917
4. Odawara Hotel, Odawara, 1917
5. Arinobu Fukuhara House, Hakone, 1918
6. Viscount Tadashiro Inoue House, Tokyo, 1918
7. Mihara House, Tokyo, 1918
8. Motion Picture Theater, Tokyo, 1918
9. Tazaemon Yamamura House, Ashiya, 1918
10. Imperial Hotel Annex, Tokyo, 1920
11. Baron Shinpei Goto House, Tokyo, 1921
12. Jiyu Gakuen School of the Free Sprit, Tokyo, 1921

Some more buildings could be added such as the house of Kodo Shugyo, Hibiya Triangle Building, and the office of Primer Minister.
Wright's works overseas including proposed plans are only about, and more than 12 of them are in Japan. Just 9 works are realized; 6 in Japan and 3 in Canada.
Existing Wright's works overseas are merely 4, all of which are in Japan (Imperial Hotel, House of Aisaku Hayashi, Former Yamamura House and Jiyu Gakuen School Myonichikan). From these facts too, we can tell how the former Yamamura house is of a particular value.

Inheriting Wright's Heritage

Masami Tanigawa

Hiding in Residential Areas

Jiyu Gakuen Myonichikan is 500 m away and 10 minutes on foot from Ikebukuro Station, one of Tokyo's subcenters. Although the areas around the station is very crowded with skyscrapers, the building site, only 500 m away , is in a quieter residential area. They say it used to be possible to see Myonichikan in the wooded area of Musashino from Noboriyashiki Station (now-defunct), 1st stop of the Seibu Line. This area is no longer picturesque; all the blocks are covered with houses, winding roads and one-way traffic. When I invited American researchers on Wright to Myonichikan, they were always surprised and would ask me in wonder where we were going. This approach, from the station to these buildings is not very elegant although it is registered as an Important Cultural Property. However, everyone is convinced that they have arrived at Myonichikan when they have the grand view of it after turning right at the junction of three streets in front of the Fujin no tomo company designed by Raku Endo, the second son of Arata Endo. People often stare in awe at the site.

The Hanis desired an economical design. The school buildings, surprisingly, have a simple atmosphere as well as a dignified elegance for child education. A U-shape plan, surrounding the spreading lawn, is a widely convincing, easy and effective method. Although such a method has been used for a number of authorized buildings, Myonichikan does not have an intimidating atmosphere of that kind. This is because the symmetric planning of the buildings does not emphasize the centrality. There are 2 gates and 4 entrances of the main buildings (2 on each side). The buildings even give us a sense of affinity because the plan is based on the principles of equality and democracy.

▶ 教員室と東教室 - 5 の外観。教員室はアトリエ - 2 と対象の位置にある。生徒たちは登下校時、ここで先生と挨拶をかわす。

Appearance of the teachers' room and the east classroom-5. The teachers' room is located symmetrical to the atelier-2. Students greet teachers there.

軽快な空間構成

　ライトの建築の妙味は、断面形の構成にある。明日館の建築は、ほとんどが平屋建て教室であるから、層を重ねる中央棟のホールや食堂の部分に、設計の妙味をみるということになろう。この重なりは、実は半階が単位。ドライエリアに半地下室、半階上にホール、さらに半階昇って食堂、その半階上にギャラリーがある。つまりここはスキップ・フロア。普通の階段数の半分で次のフロアに到達できる構成になっている。人間の行動、動作の中で、もっとも疲労度の高いのが階段の昇降だという。半階で次にフロアに達するこの構成は、疲労度を低減することに役立っている。

　明日館を通していえることだが、建具の全てが扉である。戸は一枚もない。扉が回転、戸が引戸。ライトが日本の戸や襖や障子に興味を持っていたことは、彼の著書「自叙伝」などの記述によって解っているが、建築の設計に引戸を使うことはなかった。すべてが回転扉（出入口も窓も）である。建具の中で、４カ所だけフラッシュ扉（自由蝶番による、押しても引いても開閉可能な扉）が使われている。廊下とホール、廊下と厨房の出入口、東西に１カ所づつ。このフラッシュ扉が取り付けられている部分は、極めて使用頻度が高い。出来ることなら取り外したいような部分である。そして、食堂への出入口に扉はない。

　畳を基準尺度として展開する和風の建築は、ライトに深い感銘を与えた。６帖の間、８帖の間などと広さのみ規制されたそれぞれの部屋は、いわば無目的的であり、しかし多目的的である。使い勝手は使い手が決める。２つの部屋の境界となっている襖や障子を取り払えば、さらに大きい空間が確保できる。そうしたフレキシブルな空間に魅せられたライトは、ホール、食堂、厨房を隣接させ、層状に重ねて、ドラマチックな空間を醸成した。一つにまとまった各部屋は、連続して流動する空間となる。軽快でリズミカルでもあるここは、ライトが演出した空間のハイライトといえる。

ホールと同じ高さの廊下から階段を半階昇れば食堂に、半階降りれば厨房に繋がる。ライトは平面上の空間の持続性の他に、高さの異なる部屋の連続性にも配慮した。

The dining room is a half stair case higher and the kitchen is half a stair case lower from the hallway at the level of the hall. Wright paid attention to the continuity of rooms of different levels, not only to the continuity of rooms on the same floor.

中央棟教室を結ぶ廊下。ここには列柱などない。それぞれの部分は細やかなデザインで統一されている。

Hallway connecting the classrooms of the main buildings. Here is no row of columns. Each part has a synthesized and detailed design.

Swinging Spatial Composition

廊下から縦に長い窓を通して教
室を見る。細心の心遣いが詩情
豊かな雰囲気を醸し出す。

*Looking at the classroom from
the hallway through a
vertically long window. Great
attention creates a poetic
atmosphere.*

The hidden charm of Wright's architecture lies in the sectional composition. Because most buildings of Myonichikan are one-story classrooms, we can find this kind of planning at the layered hall or the dining room of the main building. The unit of these layers, actually, is half a story. From the bottom to the top, there are the basement floor, the half-basement floor, the hall, the dining room and the gallery and each room is located at a level difference of half a story. That is, split-level. We can access the next floor only with a half stair as compared with the usual staircases. They say going up and down the stairs is the most exhausting of human actions. This composition, where we can approach to the next floor with only half a length of staircase, reduces fatigue.

All the doors of Myonichikan are pivoted doors. There are no sliding doors at all. It is known from descriptions in such as Wright's "autobiography" that he was interested in Japanese sliding doors (including *shoji* and *fusuma*). Yet, he had not used sliding doors in his architectural planning. All the doors and windows had been revolving ones. Among all the fittings of Myonichikan, only 4 are flush doors, which we can both push and pull to open. These are the doors between the hallway and the hall and between the hallway and the kitchen, both in the east and west. These flush doors are frequently open and shut. We would like to get rid of these doors, if possible. There is no door at the entrance to the dining room.

Japanese architecture, developing with *tatami* mat as a basic module, impressed Wright deeply. Such rooms of "6 tatami mats" or "8 *tatami* mats," defined only by their largeness, are multi-purpose as well as no-purpose. Users decide the usability of these rooms. In addition, we can create a larger space by getting rid of the sliding doors between these rooms. Wright, fascinated by such a flexible space, fostered a dramatic space by neighboring and layering the hall, the dining room and the kitchen. Each room, combined as one, becomes a continuous and fluid space. This space, light and rhythmical as well, would be the highlight of Wright's spatial direction.

細部に眼を向ける。窓には控えめな装飾が施されて、光彩を放っている。本来ならば、ステンド・グラスで装飾されるはずの建具に、窓の桟や枠や幾何学的な飾りを付け、あるいは、ベニヤ板を貼って、光を透して見るという…。照明器具は、ホール、ギャラリー、玄関などにランタンボックスが幾何学的なデザインを施されて東西に同じ数だけ設けられる。トップライトやダウンライトも常に東西に同じ数…。食堂に吊られたペンダントや小食堂のシーリングライトなどは、それ自体芸術作品である。

　明日館の建築は、全体構想から細部に至るまで、芸術性の高い造形への腐心によって成立しており、ライトのその設計態度に感動させられる。

　もっとも、ライトの執念とも思える造形へのこだわりの故か、いささか不思議な造形もある。例えば、西教室棟に建つ煙突の真下には、確かに大谷石を配した暖炉があるのだが、東教室棟の煙突の真下には、暖炉の痕跡すらないといったこと。あるいは、食堂の四隅に、天井からつられた箱型が壁に張り付いている。食堂に入るとき、頭が若干押さえられ、食堂をより広く、より高く感じさせるための細工なのだが、箱形のどこにも開閉装置がなく、盲に伏せられている。また、外観上や内壁との関わり方の故にか、棒高跳びのポールさえ収納できる、奥深い物入れがあったりと、ライト自身が楽しみながら、悩みながら設計を進めたような節もある。

食堂の燠炉。その上部にはビルト・インの棚が設けられている。半階下されたホールの燠炉と背中合わせの位置に設置。

Fireplace of the dining room. There is a built-in shelf above. This is back on to the fireplace of the hall a half stair case down from this room.

Details. The shiny decorations of the window are modest. The opening, which otherwise might be decorated with stained glass, penetrates light with geometrically decorated sash bars and boarded plywood. Regarding lighting equipment, geometrically designed lantern boxes are set in the hall, the gallery, the entrance and so on. The same number of the boxes are on both the east and west sides. Upper and lower lightings also exist equally on the both sides. The pendant lighting in the dining room and the ceiling lighting in the small dining rooms are works of art in themselves.

The Myonichikan architecture is made of the struggle for aesthetic designs; from the master plan to the details. Such a design attitude of Wright is impressive.

On the contrary, maybe because of his strong obsessions, there are some strange designs. For example, although there is a fireplace at the bottom right of the chimney in the west classroom building, there is no trace of a fireplace at the bottom of the chimney of the east classroom building. Another example would be the boxes at the four corners of the dining room ceiling. These are gimmicks to make us feel the dining room is larger with the smaller entrance. There is no opening to these boxes. There is, moreover, an extremely deep storage space even for vaulting poles probably because of the relation between the outer appearance and the inner walls. There are, hence, some hints that Wright enjoyed and suffered designing this school.

伝統工法とライト

　架構式工法を伝承してきた日本に、ライトは組積式工法を伝承する国からやってきた。そして、彼はついぞ日本で架構式の建築を遺さなかった、ということは興味深い。木材という長大材が容易に得られた日本と、石や煉瓦を丹念に積み上げて、建物の壁体を築き上げる彼地の工法との違いである。

　架構式は原則的に真壁造り、そして、組積式は大壁造りに仕上げられる。

　具体的にいえば、工事半ばで早々と挙行される「上棟式」という儀式。これは架構式の建物の場合に限って行われ、組積式の建物では行われることがない。「上棟式」は、屋根を支える骨格が組み終わったことを祝う行事である。柱や梁、小屋の組み物などは、すべて構造材。式後引き続いて行われる工事は、化粧材（あるいは雑作材）の取り付け作業である。化粧材は、原則的に屋根を支える責から免除される。つまり、それぞれの部材の機能分化が確立しているのである。

　また、柱や梁で保障された壁を柱の太さより薄いものとするのが通例なので、視覚的プライバシーは保障されたが、聴覚的なそれは期待できない構造である。しかし、静謐な生活を志す学校にはあっていたのかもしれない。

　組積式工法は、機能は未分化、全体主義的な工法で、築かれた壁全体で屋根蓋を支えるという方式。出来得る限り軽量化した屋根蓋を、ソーッと壁体に載せるというのが、もっとも安全な構築の方法なのである。明日館の屋根が瓦棒葺きとなっているのは、そのためである。あの重量感のある帝国ホテルも瓦棒葺きの屋根を持っているが、その小屋組みが木造で軽量化に寄与していたことは、あまり知られていない。

　自由学園の屋根蓋は、4寸勾配（寸という単位を使っているが、尺貫法で説明しようというわけではない。水平距離1尺に対して4寸高さが増すという、屋根勾配を示す指示法。古来わが国で一般的なこと。メートル法でいえば、1m進んで40cm高くなるのと同じ）、比較的緩やかな勾配で軽快感がある。

　彼はこの屋根勾配とほとんど同じ勾配の天井を多用している。いわゆる舟底天井である。低い天井の廊下から、勾配のある天井の部屋に入ると、実寸以上の高さを感じて開放感を体験することになる。ライトはこうしたドラマチックな造形手法を多用して、それぞれの部屋に生気を吹き込んだ。こうして造られた部屋の一体感を計るために、壁も天井も漆喰塗り仕上げと

● 中央棟と東教室棟の外観

Appearance of the main building and the east classroom building

Traditional Construction Methods and Wright

Wright came from the USA, where masonry construction is passed on, to Japan, where skeleton construction is handed down. It is interesting he did not create architecture of skeleton construction in Japan. It is a difference between Japan, where it is easy to obtain large wooden materials, and the USA, where they build up stone or brick to create walls.

Skeleton construction basically adopts half-timber walls while masonry construction adopts stud walls.

In concrete, *Jotoshiki*, a roof-raising ceremony is only used for skeleton construction buildings, not for masonry construction. *Jotoshiki* is to celebrate the completion of the structure supporting a roof.

All columns, beams and roof trusses are structural members. After *Jotoshiki*, the following work is to attach dressed lumbers. Dressed lumbers are not responsible for supporting a roof. That is, functions of each part are separated.

In addition, walls, secured by columns and beams, are generally thinner than the width of columns. Acoustic privacy is, therefore, not expected to be kept, while visional privacy is secured. However, such a lack of acoustic privacy may not have been a problem at the school aimed at a serene life.

Masonry construction is totalistic with undifferentiated functions and all walls are used to support the roof. The safest construction method is to carefully put a roof of a minimized weight on the top of walls. That is why the roof of Myonichikan is tiled. The massive Imperial Hotel has a tiled roof, but it is not well known that its wooden roof truss contributed to the weight saving of the roof.

The roof of Jiyu Gakuen School has a slope of 40cm/1m, which is relatively moderate.

Wright frequently adopts the ceilings of almost the same slope as this roofing slope. That is, "ship's hull ceiling." We would feel a height and openness of space more than the actual measurement when entering from a low-ceiling room to a sloping-ceiling room. Wright vitalized each room frequently with such dramatic design methods. Both the walls and the ceilings are finished with stucco to keep a sense of unity of the rooms created that way. The roof, hence, increased its weight more than expected. The walls, supporting the roof, slightly start opening to the outside. The walls had cracks and rain water penetrated, and the roof started leaking. Degradation proceeded.

Wright mainly created buildings with stud walls in Japan. Wood materials with a square section are then unnecessary for columns because they will be hidden beneath wall paintings. Wood materials of half or 1/3 size was enough. Wooden structure of Myonichikan has a

大地と繋がる力は

多様化という形で運ばれるのは、明日開く稼業の稼業の花の質も問題である。

ライトは、大地と調和してその生を再び蘇らせ、緑の米と土地のいくつもの「高度様式」の作業を選んだ。学校建築であるけれども、彼は回りにものがたる。これは緑が繋がり織りなす、すぐに劣化化した痕。

現象を変えてみる。われわれの目は有効長さ10cm下からった がある。どうかも知れない。

ところにある。隣が横に向いていて、その奥らの半世界が広がり の世界に生きている。

車の窓からの祖母を子供に説明している。子供は「どこ?」 とうち上がって、隣の様子をする様子、親と子供は有長の姉は の世界に生きている。

左手が末端表の淡から睡眠を蕈苗は、苗ぽから成ったしたれば、 ライトの小植いほかの経理種度というこにとらわれるなら な。こんな植えをしてても、ライトの草の種の繊維には繁がるる。 い。乾燥した環境と養分の多い砂地では、床が湿ら を喰って、植物の養分を補給しているという。

たちなければよいとなら喘ぐ。

ある。その2×4が正角の明日買いの明日買で使われていた、再調に りがりキャチャの工場をの工場を種植的に様用しようと繋めたことが 選構造体は、周期的に2×4。大樓範囲らなく日本では、アメ てこの半分、あるいは、3分の1の木材が重要あり、明日買の木 種に達り込められたち様に、正方形断面の木材などは一変。すべ ライトは日本に来て、単なる植木作りの植物作りを選んだ。 種針化は進行していたのである。

種面に電線が発生して、用水が浸透入、廃水するようになった。 した。種畜化を測りて過られた間横範は、予種を繋えて重害を重畳 した。間横範の荷重を考えようとれた繋がざ右に開きはじめる。

中央棟西教室−１と教室への玄関。中央棟の南部分には一ル６織彫と大谷石の花置きーポッチがほどこされている。

Main building west classroom-1 and entrance to the classroom. There are flower boxes of Oya stone installed at the south part of the main building and the same kind of boxes in front of the hall and the classrooms.

basic section of 2x4 (inch). Once the USA and Canada attempted to widely adopt this construction method soon after WWII. It is surprising that the 2x4 method was already used at Myonichikan during the preceding Taisho period (1912-1926).

Floors Connected to the Ground

What is associated with degradation is the floor level of the classrooms of Myonichikan.

Wright created a "Prairie House" seemingly integrated with and growing out of the ground. It is said he made the floor level of the Myonichikan classrooms equal to the ground level so that the building will be connected to the ground although it is school architecture, not a Prairie House. This anecdote has been passed on and seems like the accepted theory at present. Maybe so.

From another perspective. Our eyes are about 10 cm below the top of our body. Our eyelids are horizontally long and we live in the world of planar expansion at that level.

When explaining the scenery from the window of a train to a child, the child stands up to ask "where?" and looks at the direction the parents are pointing. Parents and children live in different worlds from a difference of body heights.

It might be because of this exquisite design attitude of Wright that Myonichikan schoolgirls saw from the classroom windows only blue sky. Such an assumption would not advocate the disadvantages of Wright's architecture. In humid Japan, different from the dry States, the floors absorb humidity and the life of the building is shortened.

意志を継ぐ弟子

　道路の南側に建設された講堂は、弟子の遠藤新の設計による
ものである。もし、ライトが急遽帰国するという事態に遭遇す
ることなく、この講堂の設計を依頼されたとすれば、こういう
形にまとめるに違いない作品を、遠藤は造ったといえる。短期
間の内に、遠藤はライトの設計手法を習得していたということ
の証明。遠藤の講堂は、明日館の３棟の建築と渾然一体となり、
ライトの意図を損ねることはない。講堂の建築は、ライトの工
房タリアセンの風情を彷彿させる。
　日本大学工学部の私の研究室では、ライトの日本での業績の
調査研究に、卒業研究の学生と取り組んできた。彼の作品の実
測図を造ろうと、最初に実践したのが「自由学園」であった。
1971年のことである。これを皮切りに「旧林邸」、「旧山邑邸」、
さらに京都大学建築学教室に保存されている「銀座に建つ映画

Apprentice Inheriting Wright's' heritage.

The auditorium in the south across the street was designed by Arata Endo, Wright's apprentice. Endo created what Wright should have created if he had been asked to design the auditorium before leaving Japan. This may be the evidence that Endo learned Wright's design methods during only a short term. The auditorium by Endo has a sense of integrity with the 3 buildings of Myonichikan and does not spoil Wright's intention. The auditorium architecture reminds us of Wright's workshop, Taliesin.

In my laboratory at the College of Engineering, Nihon University, we have implemented research on Wright's achievements in Japan for our students' graduation theses. We chose "Jiyu Gakuen school" first when we tried to have a measurement survey to draw the plans of his works. It was in 1971. We then measured "House of Aisaka Hayashi",

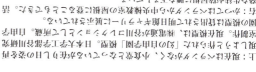

Above: "Unrealized Jiyu Gakuen School" model. This was made to visualize the buildings of the past although there are small dining rooms instead of verandahs. By Tanigawa Laboratory, Nihon University. This model now belongs to the Tanigawa Collection, Dentsu Inc. The model of Jiyu Gakuen School is rented and displayed at the Myonichikan gallery.
Right: They could go up the roof of the classrooms of the main building from the verandah. Active students are seated on the flat roof.

上：遠景はベランダをあるく、小者達を見ているLDの客と見えしようと作られた。日本大学工学部谷川研究室制作。現在模型は、株電通谷川コレクションとして保蔵。自由学園の模型は貸出されて明日館ギャラリーに展示されている。
右：クラスルームから中央棟屋根の屋根に登ることもできた。活発な生徒は解放屋根に腰を下ろしている。

Left: There are big doors to the verandah on the east and west of the dining room of the main building at the time of completion.

左：中央棟竣工時東、西面には、ベランダに出る大きな開き戸が付いていた。

Left: Founders of the Jiyu Gakuen School,
The Hanis (Yoshikazu and Motoko).
Right page, left: The opening ceremony of
the school was held in the west classroom-2
of the main building on the April 15th 1921
and the walls were just undercoated.
Right page, right: Walls of the classroom
were scraped during the restoration work.

左：学園創設者、羽仁もと子夫妻。
右左：1921年（大正10）4月15日、小学棟
西教室-2で開校式が行われたが、壁は下塗
りの状態であった。
右右：保存復原工事で壁が削がれた教室。

巨匠への憧憬

明治時代後期の頃、当時は未だほとんど世界に紹介されていなかった帝国大学教授

羽仁もと子は、1901年（明治34）、回覧雑誌の走りとも言える「家庭之友」、続いてもと子は、2年後、もと子は夫・吉一とともに「婦人之友」に改題」して、家庭婦人への啓蒙運動を開始した。

羽仁もと子は、この個人運動雑誌の経営の中で、子女教育の重要性に着目し、1920年（大正9）になって女子学校を設立を決意した。時代は、大正へと推移していた。

子女教育の羽仁夫妻の行動は迅速であった。学園に通う家族に

それは、1921年（大正10）1月のある日。天津は帝国ホテルを訪

自由学園中小学棟尾張部の紋様から工事が始まり、中小学棟、西尾張棟、東尾張棟の順に工事が進行した。しかし、東尾張棟が着工する以前に、春雄の図版という重要な資料が、3万枚の少年建工するまでのすべての復原工事が終了した
に、3つの小屋裏などないというこの模様は、「幻」の自由学園」。そして、ライトの設計原図を基礎づける貴重な資料という

とになった。

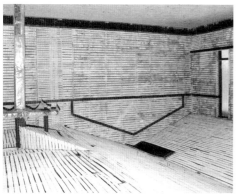

"Yamamura House" and the model of "Movie Theater in Shibuya" kept at the Faculty of Architecture, Kyoto University. We collected all the project plans. We then began making housing models based on the measured drawings; all in 1/100 scale. We did not start making models except for houses, because there was not enough space for storage. However, urged by the students, we launched into making a model of "Unrealized Jiyu Gakuen School" when we came to realize that the site of Jiyu Gakuen School is actually smaller than that of other houses.

The construction of Jiyu Gakuen School started with the classrooms of the west end of the main building, then proceeded to the other parts of the main building, the west classroom building and the east classroom building lastly. However, before the completion of the east classroom building, the annex of the dining room was demanded and the 3 small dining rooms were constructed. That is why the model is called "Unrealized Jiyu Gakuen School" that has all the buildings including the east classroom building without the 3 small dining rooms. It is said that it would be precious data to reaffirm Wright's original design purposes.

Request for a Maestro of Architecture

It was in the late Meiji period. Motoko Matsuoka, a female newspaper reporter, who was still rare in those days, married to Yoshikazu Hani, her colleague newspaper reporter and resigned from the newspaper publishing company in 1901. Two years later, Motoko and Yoshikazu published the first issue of "*Katei no tomo*," meaning family's friend (later changed to "*Shufu no tomo*," meaning women's friend) to commence the enlightenment of domestic women.

Motoko Hani focused on child education through the promotion of the women's movement. She decided to establish a girls' school in

完成期に行われた落成式

慌ただしい日々であったとはいえ、桜花の落慶工事は
引き続いて行われる。

1922年（大正11）2月18日には医療衛生棟の建築が始まり、同
年4月には中央棟がほぼ完成。そして、6月9、10回には目白
学園の落成式が挙行された。このため式には、ライト邸遠藤と
並びに、落成記念にちなむられたライトの「目白荘園の建築」
は、遠藤の設えた共に『婦人之友』同年6月号に掲載された。

その次の目白荘園にちなんで目白が来たこと、北の小から
幸福なる子女の、職業にしてからを業しる園。からなる
多様の意匠の瀟洒なものであります。

……一年程はしかにも、桜が次にいただいた花に見えます。また
来る春だ。……
花が来る一つ。そのうちに、桜も芽を伸ばすように。

ライトがこの学校建築に注いだ情熱と自信のほどを窺わせる
ことが出来る。

1922年の目白荘園

This photo was taken on 1922.

着工中のフランク・ロイド・ライトの事務所を訪ねて、桜花
桜花会の設計を依頼する。1月22日には、ライトの設計が完成
の下に譲れ、2月15日には主要な建物がライトに委ねられた
ようには、遠藤が建築者としている。さらに、3月15日には、建築
を譲り受ける目白荘園本体は開校とともに、同日正式発足までに
を譲り受ける足工棟居が着工を開始。そして、4月15日や着工棟か
の目白荘園は完成したのである。もっとも、この桜花の落成式い
はまだ桜谷が完成したのといい、取り取らず開校に間に合わせた
のである。中かは建築関係
の1桜谷が出来上がったといってよかった。年は桜谷26名という
少規模な学校は、こうして開校したのだった。開校とともに予定
様子する姿もある。間に合わない桜谷という教の桜谷は落慶り
の桜谷は4月22日に着工、5月4日に完成して、遅日の奉祝入
学式に間に合った。

一方、「目白荘園の創立」主たる『婦人之友』に掲載された
学校を開校に合わせている。

であり、東京府知事宛に設立認可に係る書面が提出されたのは、3
も実質的な生徒募集が続けられたのは、同年2月6号を羅列上において
8月24日のことであった。

1920. It was then in the Taisho period.

The Hanis acted quickly once they decided what to do. On a day in January 1921, they visited the office of Frank Lloyd Wright working on the construction of the Imperial Hotel. They asked Wright to design buildings for a girls' school. Wright visited the planned construction site on January 22nd. The contract was already concluded when the Hanis visited the hotel to see Wright on February 15th. Accordingly on March 15th, Mera builder's office started the construction. By noon of April 15th, almost all the school buildings were completed for the opening ceremony of the regular course of Jiyu Gakuen School held on that day. The completion of the school buildings here is, precisely, only one classroom at the west end of the main building to be finished in time for the opening ceremony of the school. That is the way the small school with 26 students was opened. There is a photograph of Mrs. Hani making a speech at the ceremony. The "completed" walls of the classroom were rough coated and a plumb is pinned with a nail. The classroom next to it was started on April 22nd and completed on May 4th to be in time for the opening ceremony of the advanced course the next day.

It was in the February edition of "Fujin no tomo" that the concepts of "establishment of Jiyu Gakuen School" was posted and the recruiting of students was practically commenced. The application for an incorporation approval was submitted to the governor of Tokyo on March 24th.

Completion Ceremony before the Completion

Although the commencement was in a rush, the construction of the school buildings was implemented consecutively.

The construction of the west classroom building was begun on February 18th 1922 and the main building was almost finished in April. The completion ceremony of Jiyu Gakuen School was, accordingly, held on June 9th and 10th. Wright as well as Endo attended this ceremony. Wright extended his congratulations for the opening of the school by sending a message and it was posted with Endo's translation in the June edition of "Fujin no tomo."

"This little school building was designed for the "Jiyu" Gakuen - in the same spirit implied by the name of the school - a free spirit. The children seem to belong to the building in quite the same way as the flowers belong to the tree, and the building belongs to them as the tree belongs to its flowers."

The passion and confidence of Wright for these school buildings are expressed here.

実は、ライトが描いた設計図は中央棟と西教室棟のみ。東教室棟は描かれていない。しかし、この建築群の設計構想は予め決まっていた。3,000m²強（1,000坪にもみたない、約900坪）という限られた敷地の、道路に面する南側に、可能な限り広い芝生の庭が設定される。そのために、中央棟は道路から奥まった北側に、そして、中央棟と直交する西教室棟と東教室棟は、それぞれ隣地境界線一杯に後退した位置に建設される。原則的に左右対称の構成。中央棟のホールと食堂が2階の高さに仕上げられる他、各教室は平屋建。この地を這うような造形は、ライトが若くして確立した草原住宅（プレーリー・ハウス）のスタイルを彷彿させる学園が誕生するのだと。この構想に基づけば、未だ東教室棟が完成をみない時期に早々と落成式が挙行されたことになる。

残された図面と未完の校舎

1922年（大正11）の春、帝国ホテルで最悪の事態が発生する。

4月16日の午後、渡辺譲設計になる初代帝国ホテルの地下室から出火、全焼した。しかも、宿泊者の1人が焼死し、負傷者も23人に及んだ。この事態を受けて、翌日重役会で善後策が講じられ、さらに3日後の4月20日に開催された重役会で、取締役会長大倉喜八郎以下取締役全員が、ホテル全焼の責任をとって、辞表を提出した。ライトのホテル建設を支持し、擁護してきた大倉男爵も支配人林愛作も、ホテルの経営陣から姿を消した。

度重なる工費の膨張、工期の遅滞の責任がライトにのしかかり、罷免は避けられない事態となった。「罷免」とは穏やかでない。『帝国ホテル百年史』には、次のように記されている。

「大正11年7月12日、新ホテル建築関係者が招集され…」
「この会合において、ライトが帰国を声明（7月7日）したことが明らかにされた。」

とあり、この声明については、翌7月13日の重役会で、「ライトは『7月22日に帰米する』と大倉会長に言明し、これに対し大倉会長は、『帝国ホテルとしてこれを拝承する』と口答で答えた」と説明されたという。日本流の「武士の情」ということか。ここに登場する「大倉会長」というのは、新しい経営陣の会長、

帝国ホテル
東京、1912年。
撮影：谷川正己©
ライトは竣工を見ずに帰国したが出来上がった一室を東京の事務所として使用した。
もっともしばしば事務所を訪ねたのは設計依頼の人々ではなくて浮世絵を売りたいバイヤーだったというエピソードがある。

The Imperial Hotel
Tokyo, 1912.
Photo: Masami Tanigawa©
Although Wright left Japan before the completion, he used a room of the hotel as his Tokyo office.
There is, however, an anecdote that those who often visited the office were not his clients, but buyers with a purpose of selling Ukiyoe to him.

The plans drawn by Wright are, actually, the ones for the main building and the west classroom building. There is not any for the east classroom building. The design concept for these 3 buildings, was already decided. In the limited site of a bit more than 3,000m2, a grass lawn would be created as large as possible on the south along the street. The main building would be, therefore, constructed in the north a little far from the street. The west and east classroom buildings, right across the main building, would be set right on the site borderline. Basically using a symmetric composition, each classroom is one story except for the hall and the dining room which are two stories. This design, as if crawling on the ground, reminds us of Prairie House style, which Wright achieved in his younger days. The school was based on such a concept. The completion ceremony was held earlier when the east building was not yet completed.

Left Drawings and Unfinished School Buildings

One of the worst cases happened at the Imperial Hotel in the spring of 1922.

There was a fire in the basement floor of the first Imperial Hotel, designed by Yuzuru Watanabe, and it burned all the building. What was worse was that a guest was burned to death and 23 people were injured. Following this, there was a board meeting the next day and, accordingly 3 days later, all the board members including the board chairperson Kihachiro Okura submitted their resignation to take responsibility of the burnout of the hotel. Baron Okura and the chief manager Aisaku Hayashi, who had supported and advocated for Wright in the construction of the hotel, left the top management.

Wright became responsible for repeated increases of construction fees and the delay of construction. A dismissal would be inescapable. "Dismissal" sounds too much. "100 year history of the Imperial Hotel" goes as follows;

"Those who were concerned with the construction of the new hotel gathered on July 12th 1923…"
"It was proclaimed Wright's leaving Japan on July 7th."

The statement was said to be explained at the next board meeting on July 13th: 'Wright declared "leaving for the USA on July 22nd" to the board chairperson Okura and he answered the "the Imperial Hotel is honored to accept that." It might have been the Japanese way to show mercy. The "board chairperson Okura" here refers to the new chairperson of the board, Kishichiro Okura, son of the former chairperson Kihachiro.

林愛作邸
東京、1917年。帝国ホテルの支
配人だった林の自邸。
Aisaku Hayashi House
Tokyo, 1917. Residence for Hayashi, the manager of the Imperial Hotel.

大倉喜七郎（前会長喜八郎の息子）を指している。

　ライトの突然の帰国表明は、自由学園の建設工事にも影響が及ぶ。帝国ホテルの全館完成を見ることなく帰国することになったライトが、遠藤新らに「南翼は北翼と同じに建てればよい」と言い残してわが国を離れたことはよく知られている。自由学園の場合も、ホテルとまったく同じパターン。ライトは弟子たちに、「東教室棟は西教室棟と同じに建てればよい」と指示して、7月22日に横浜港から帰国した。ライトは、その後再びわが国の土を踏むことは無かった。

　遠藤は、ライトの指示通り、西教室棟の図面を裏返しにして、1925年（大正14）までに東教室棟を竣工させた。それより前、1923年（大正12）から翌年にかけて、手狭になった食堂の増築も遠藤が行っている。食堂の東西両端と北側中央部に小食堂を設置して、生徒数の増加に対応した。さらに、道路の南側の敷地に講堂が建設されて、すべての建築が建ち揃った。設計は遠藤新。1927年（昭和2）1月26日に起工、同年6月18日に落成式が挙行された。中央棟ホールを講堂に兼用していたが、テニス用の運動場の敷地に専用の講堂が完成したのだった。

昭和の文化財指定第一号

旧山邑邸（現・淀川製鋼所迎賓館）1924年

Yamamura House
(Yodoko Guest House) 1924

　すべての建築が建ち揃った学園だが、敷地の狭隘は発展の障害となっていた。新しい広大な敷地を入手することは、学園にとって急務であった。学園の移転計画は1925年（大正14）から始められる。池袋西郊、北多摩郡久留米村南沢に10万坪の土地を購入して、校地と分譲住宅地を確保。学園の父母らに住宅地分譲を開始。その利益で新校舎が建設される。この新校舎への移転は、1930年（昭和5）に始まり、1934年（昭和9）には全学部の移転が終了した。これを契機に学園発祥の建築群は「明日館」と名付けられ、引き続き教学施設として使用され続ける。

　自由学園明日館は1997年（平成9）5月29日に、国指定の重要文化財となり、1999年（平成11）1月より38ヶ月をかけて半解体工事が行われ、2002年（平成14年）2月に工事が完了。1927年（昭和2）当時の麗姿に蘇った。1927年というのは、明日館のすべての建築が建ち揃った年、ライト設計の中央棟、西教室棟、東教室棟をはじめ、遠藤新設計の中央棟に増築された三方の小食堂、講堂も含まれる。

　ライトがわが国に遺した業績、旧山邑邸（現・淀川製鋼所迎

This sudden declaration of Wright influenced the construction work of Jiyu Gakuen School. It is well known that Wright, when he left Japan before the completion of the Imperial Hotel, said to Arata Endo "the south wing can be made as same as the north wing". It was exactly the same regarding Jiyu Gakuen School. Wright told his apprentices "the east classroom building can be made as same as the west classroom building" and left Japan from the Yokohama port on July 22nd. He never returned to Japan again.

Endo completed the east classroom building by 1925 by tuning back the drawing of the west classroom building as Wright told him. Earlier than that, he also conducted the annex of the dining room from 1923 to the next year. The small dining rooms were added to the east and west ends and the central part of the dining room to deal with the increase of students. The auditorium designed by Arata Endo constructed in the south site across the street and all the buildings were finished. The auditorium was commenced on January 26th and the completion ceremony was held on June 18th. Until then, they used the hall of the main building as an auditorium too, and the exclusive auditorium was finished in the tennis field site.

First Registration as a Cultural Property in the Showa Period

The smallness of the land area prevented the school from development even after the buildings were all completed. It was an urgent task for the school to obtain a new larger site. A transfer plan of the school started in 1925. The school bought a site of about 340,000 m2 in Minamisawa, Kurume, Kitatama in the west suburb of Ikebukuro. The school site and land for ready-built houses were reserved there. The school started selling ready-built houses for the parents of the students. With the benefits, the new school buildings were constructed. This transfer began in 1930 and all the faculties were finished by 1934. At this transfer, architecture of the school origin was named Myonichikan and was still used for education.

Jiyu Gakuen School Myonichikan was registered as an Important Cultural Property by the government on May 29th 1997. Restoration work was conducted for about 38 months from January 1999. The architecture regained the beauty of its birth. 1927 was the year when all the buildings of Myonichikan were completed; the main building, the west and east classroom buildings designed by Wright and the small 3 dining annexes and the auditorium designed by Arata Endo.

Yamamura House (Yodoko Guest House), another work by Wright, was registered as Important Cultural Property in 1974. Myonichikan became the 2nd registration 23 years later. The

賓館）が重要文化財に指定されたのは1974年のこと。それから23年後に明日館が2件目の指定ということになるのだが、旧山邑邸の場合が大正期建設の指定第一号であった。同じように、明日館の場合は昭和期建設の講堂が昭和期の指定第一号ということになった。質の高い建築は年代を超えて保存されなければならないという、文化財行政の片鱗をみる想いがする。

動態保存への試み

「明日館」の文化財指定では、新しい手法が試みられることになった。「動態保存」の実践である。これは、未だ機能が消滅していない場合に実行できることである。

そういえば、「明日館」は実に長く使用され続けたと思う。1921年の学園創設から1934年の全学部の南沢キャンパスへの移転完了まで、学園の校舎として使用されたのは13年、あまりにも短期間で所期の目的を終えたのだった。しかし、その後も工芸研究所、消費経済研究部、卒業生会事務局、それに婦人之友社分室などの活動に利用されてきた。学園にとって利を生まない、維持費の嵩む明日館は厄介なお荷物。売却、建て替え、幾つかの解決策を検討しながら、結論は先延ばし。紆余曲折の時日は半世紀にも及んだ。

1994年（平成6）7月14日、自由学園は「明日館専門家委員会」を開催した。私はこの委員会のメンバーの1人として会に出席した。要件は絞り込まれていた。「明日館」を残すか、残さないか。最終判断をすることが目的であった。委員会は翌年1月12日、同年12月11日の計3回開催された。種々討議を重ねた中で、オブザーバーとして出席された文化庁文化財調査官の発言は、印象的なものであった。文化財行政の指向が格段に改善されつつあることを知ったからである。長過ぎた結論の先延ばしは、学園にとって幸いなこととなった。学園が想い描いていた文化財指定を受けると、多くの規制や拘束で身動きできなくなるという不安は杞憂であった。時が追い風となった。

結論は、文化財指定を受けて「明日館」を使い続けるというのであった。当時の学園長羽仁翹氏（故人）の決断に、拍手をおくった。吉岡努明日館長（現・明日館名誉館長）の東奔西走の尽力も忘れられない。

● 学園創立10周年記念のフレスコ画を描く生徒たち。

This mural was painted by students on 1931.

auditorium of Myonichikan was the first registration in the *Showa* period, while Yamamura House was the first in the *Taisho* period. It might have reflected a glimpse of the Cultural Agency's administrative policy that high-quality architecture should be preserved beyond time.

Trial for Dynamic Conservation

A new method was attempted in the registration of Myonichikan as a Cultural Property. Practical "dynamic conservation." It can be completed when functions still exist.

In that connection, Myonichikan was used for such a long time. The use of these buildings as a school was, on the other hand, only for 13 years from the school establishment in 1921 to the transfer of all the faculties to Minamisawa campus in 1934. The buildings were used since then as a polytechnic institute, a laboratory of consumers economy, an administrative office of alumni and a satellite office of Fujin no tomo company. Myonichikan was a troublesome burden for the school, which was not an economic benefit and was costly to maintain. The school searched for solutions such as selling or renovating. Conclusions were not drawn. Such ups and downs continued for about half a century.

Jiyu Gakuen School held the "Specialist Committee on Myonichikan" on July 14th 1994. I, as a member of the committee, attended the meeting. The issue was succinct. To keep or not to keep Myonichikan. The purpose of the meeting was to make the final decision. Meetings were held 3 times including the ones on January 12th and December 11th of the next year. Impressive were the remarks of the cultural property investigator of the Cultural Agency, who was attending the meeting as an observer. We came to realize the cultural administrative directions were highly improved. The long postponements of making a decision turned out to be fortunate for the school. Although the school managers thought a registration as a Cultural Property would tie them up with a number of restrictions and regulations, it turned out to not be a problem. They had the timing right.

As a result, the school was able to use Myonichikan even after its registration as a Cultural Property. I applauded the decision of Gyo Hani (defunct person), the school director at that time. Also worthy of note is the indescribable efforts of Tsutomu Yoshioka, Myonichikan director (honorary director now).

蘇る美しい姿

　「明日館」が重要文化財指定された同じ年の11月5日には、早やばやと「明日館修理委員会」が発足。修理工事の進行に合わせて委員会が開催された。計8回、2001年6月11日で委員会は解散した。

　修理工事は1999年（平成11）1月より2002年（平成14）2月に完了した。すべてはスピーディーに進行した。「明日館修理委員会」の委員も努め、先の「明日館専門家委員会」から引き続いて委員を努めたのは、何故か私1人であった。

　修復中に、委員の間で議論をしたことが1度ある。彩色の問題についてである。竣工当時の彩色を確認出来るカラー写真は1枚もない。具体的には屋根及び窓枠が彩色されていたことは、生徒の水彩画の写生で解ったし、窓枠については古材に塗られていた塗料で確認できた。ところが、講堂の屋根や窓枠は彩色されていない。ライトは「建築材料はそれぞれ素材の性質を生かし、彩色することは怪しからぬこと」といった。講堂が彩色されていないのが何よりの証拠という反論に遭った。ライトは彩色にも随分意を注ぐ人、特に銅板に噴き出す緑青の色は好んで使ったことを説明して、彩色を実践させた。

　復原、修理は慎重に行われたように思う。修復成った「明日館」の緑青は、鮮やかに蘇り、低層であるが、副都心池袋の雑踏の衝立の役目を背負って輝いている、健気な姿を見るのは嬉しいことの一つである。

いまを生きる明日館。／A Living Architecture.

Wedding

Concert

Revitalized Beauty

"Myonichikan Restoration Committee" was organized as early as November 5th in the year when Myonichikan was registered as an Important Cultural Property. Meetings were held in accordance with the restoration work, and the committee was dissolved on June 11th after 8 meetings.

The restoration work was started from January 1999, completing in February 2002. The restoration work was progressed quickly. Somehow, I was the only member who served in both the "Myonichikan Restoration Committee" and "Myonichikan Expert Committee".

During the restoration work, the committee members had a dispute once, on a coloring issue. There is no color photograph to recognize the colors after the buildings were completed. Actually, we know from watercolor paintings of students, that the roof and the window frames were colored. Old materials of the window frames even testified to the color. However, the roof or the window frames of the auditorium were not colored. Wright said, "We should maximize the natural properties of architectural materials and too much painting should be refrained." The auditorium could be an evidence to such a theory. Since Wright was careful in coloring, the coloring in restoration was cautiously conducted. We, in particular, made sure that Wright preferably used the color of verdigris on copper plates.

The restoration work seemed to be conducted with care. Although the buildings are low-rise, the verdigris of restored Myonichikan is revived vividly and shining as a buffer in the crowd of Tokyo's skyscraping sub-center, Ikebukuro. It is a pleasure to see such a noble sight.

明日館中央棟の夜景

Night view of the main building of Myonichikan

Exhibition

Exhibition

063

Frank Lloyd Wright

Jiyu Gakuen, School of The Free Sprit

Myonichikan
Tokyo 1921

Text | 谷川正己
建築史家。1930年生まれ。1953年、大阪工業大
学建築学科卒。横浜国立大学工学部勤務を経て、
日本大学工学部の教授を務める。現在は、フラン
ク・ロイド・ライト研究室を主宰。主な著書に「フ
ランク・ロイド・ライト」(鹿島出版会)、「フラン
ク・ロイド・ライトとはだれか」(王国社)、訳書に
は「ライトの遺言」谷川睦子と共訳(彰国社)など
多数。

Text | Masami Tanigawa
Architectural Historian, born in 1930. Former professor at the
College of Engineering, Nihon University.
Now, leading the Masami Tanigawa Studio of Frank Lloyd Wright.
Author of "Frank Lloyd Wright". "Road to Taliesin", "Wright and
Japan" and others. Translation, "A Testament", "An American
Architecture", "The Living City", and others.

Photos | 宮本和義
写真家。1941年上海生まれ。1964年から建築分野、
旅分野で活動。著書に「ワールドアーキテクチャ
ー」(バナナブックス)、「近代建築再見」(エクスナ
レッジ)、「和風旅館建築の美」「古寺彩々」(JTB)、
「近代建築散歩」(小学館)など多数。

Photos | Kazuyoshi Miyamoto
Photographer
Born in Shanghai in 1941
Since 1964, he has been taking architectural and travel photographs.

編集 | 石原秀一
　　　大石雄一朗
翻訳 | 牧尾晴喜[フレーズクレーズ]©
作図 | 松尾茂生
本文デザイン | 掘井知嗣
装幀 | マルプデザイン
印刷・製本 | モリモト印刷株式会社
制作協力 | アトリエM5
　　　　自由学園明日館
　　　　婦人之友社
　　　　㈶文化財建造物保存技術協会

Chief Editor | Shuichi Isihara
Staff Editor | Yuichiro Oishi
Translation | Haruki Makio(Fraze Craze Inc.)
Drafting | Shigeki Matsuo
Design | Tomotsugu Horii
Cover Design | Malpu Design Co.,Ltd.
Printer | Morimoto Print Co.,Ltd.
Special Thanks | Atelier M5
　　　　JIyu Gakuen, School of the Free Spirit
　　　　Fujin no Tomosha
　　　　JACAM

フランク・ロイド・ライト

自由学園明日館
東京 1921

2016年6月10日　新装第1刷発行
2024年2月20日　新装第3刷発行

New Edition First printing | June 10, 2016
New Edition Third printing | February 20, 2024

編集者 | 石原秀一
発行者 | 工藤秀之
発行所 | バナナブックス
株式会社トランスビュー

Chief Editor | Shuichi Ishihara
Publisher | Hideyuki Kudo
© Banana Books
TRANSVIEW Co.,Ltd.

〒103-0013　東京都中央区日本橋人形町2-30-6
Tel. 03-3664-7334　Fax. 03-3664-7335
http://www.transview.co.jp/

2-30-6, Nihonbashi-Ningyocho Chuo-ku, Tokyo, 103-0013 Japan
Tel.+81-3-3664-7334　Fax.+81-3-3664-7335
http://www.transview.co.jp/

2016 BananaBooks, Printed in Japan
All rights reserved
ISBN978-4-902930-33-7